WITHDRAWN

D1609304

Pebble® Plus

SPORTS STARS

STARS OF FOOTBALL

by Mari Schuh

Consulting Editor: Gail Saunders-Smith, PhD

CAPSTONE PRESS
a capstone imprint

Pebble Plus is published by Capstone Press,
1710 Roe Crest Drive, North Mankato, Minnesota 56003
www.capstonepub.com

Library of Congress Cataloging-in-Publication Data
Schuh, Mari C., 1975–
  Stars of football / by Mari Schuh.
      pages cm.—(Pebble plus. sports stars)
  Includes bibliographical references and index.
  Summary: "Simple text and full-color photographs feature eight current outstanding professional football players"—
Provided by publisher.
  ISBN 978-1-4765-3961-4 (library binding)—ISBN 978-1-4765-6026-7 (ebook PDF)
1. Football players—United States—Biography—Juvenile literature. I. Title.
  GV939.A1S33 2014
  796.3320922—dc23 [B]   2013030134

Editorial Credits
Erika L. Shores, editor; Sarah Bennett, designer; Eric Gohl, media researcher; Eric Manske, production specialist

Photo Credits
AP Photo: Jim Mahoney, cover; Dreamstime: Lawrence Weslowski Jr., 5, Scott Anderson, 9; Newscom: ABACAUSA.COM/ Julian H. Gonzalez, 17, Icon SMI/Andrew Richardson, 13, Icon SMI/Ray Carlin, 7, Icon SMI/Rich Gabrielson, 15, Icon SMI/ Tony Medina, 21, Reuters/Gary Hershorn, 11, 19; Shutterstock: David Lee, 1

The author dedicates this book to her dad, who often took her to watch Minnesota Vikings training camp practices in Mankato, Minnesota, when she was growing up.

Note to Parents and Teachers

The Sports Stars set supports national social studies standards related to people, places, and culture. This book describes and illustrates stars of professional football. The images support early readers in understanding the text. The repetition of words and phrases helps early readers learn new words. This book also introduces early readers to subject-specific vocabulary words, which are defined in the Glossary section. Early readers may need assistance to read some words and to use the Table of Contents, Glossary, Read More, Internet Sites, and Index sections of the book.

Printed in China by Nordica.
1013/CA21301922
092013   007747NORDS14

 Table of Contents

The Big Game

Fans watch NFL teams take the field every week during football season. The fans cheer for their favorite star players.

NFL stands for the National Football League.

Quarterbacks

Outstanding quarterback

Drew Brees passed for

the most yards in a season.

He threw for 5,476 yards.

Aaron Rodgers is a star
quarterback. He led
the Green Bay Packers to
a Super Bowl win. He was
named that Super Bowl's MVP.

MVP stands for
Most Valuable Player.

Tom Brady has won

the Super Bowl three times.

He is one of two quarterbacks

to start in the Super Bowl

five times.

Running Backs

Arian Foster is one of

the NFL's best running backs.

His 1,616-rushing yards

topped the NFL one season.

Adrian Peterson ran for

2,097 yards in a season.

It was the second highest

rushing yards in NFL history.

He was that season's MVP.

Wide Receivers

Calvin Johnson holds
the record for the most
receiving yards in a season.
He had 1,964 yards.

Wide receiver Victor Cruz made one of the NFL's longest touchdowns. He scored a 99-yard touchdown.

Defense

Linebacker Patrick Willis
has played in the Pro Bowl
six times. He is one of
the NFL's best linebackers.

Glossary

linebacker—a defensive player who lines up behind the linemen; there are usually three or four linebackers who act as the second line of defense

pass—to throw a ball to a player who then catches it

Pro Bowl—the all-star game of the NFL

quarterback—a football player who leads the offense; quarterbacks pass the football or hand it off to a player

receiving yards—yards gained from a completed pass

record—when something is done better than anyone has ever done it before

running back—an offensive player who moves the ball by running with it down the field

rushing yards—yards gained when a player carries the ball down the field

season—a time of the year; football season starts in the fall; the NFL regular season is 17 weeks long

Super Bowl—the final championship game in the NFL season

touchdown—a six-point score in a football game; touchdowns happen when the ball is carried over the goal line

Read More

Clay, Kathryn. *Cool Football Facts*. Cool Sports Facts. Mankato, Minn.: Capstone Press, 2011.

MacRae, Sloan. *Aaron Rodgers*. Sports Heroes. New York: PowerKids Press, 2012.

Savage, Jeff. *Adrian Peterson*. Amazing Athletes. Minneapolis: Lerner Publications, 2011.

Internet Sites

FactHound offers a safe, fun way to find Internet sites related to this book. All of the sites on FactHound have been researched by our staff.

Here's all you do:

Visit *www.facthound.com*

Type in this code: 9781476539614

Super-cool stuff! Check out projects, games and lots more at **www.capstonekids.com**

23

Index

Word Count: 178
Grade: 1
Early-Intervention Level: 18